© 2018 by Tony Gardner, All Rights Reserved.
The book author Tony Gardner, retains sole
copyright to his contributions to this book.
All rights reserved. No part of this book may be
reproduced or transmitted in any form or by any
means without written permission by author.

The Blurb-provided layout designs and graphic elements are
copyright Blurb Inc. This book was created using the Blurb
creative publishing service. The book author Tony Gardner
retains sole copyright to his contributions to this book.

Reflections:
> There will be no pity party...

In the midst of trouble and signs of trouble... A dose of inspiration was needed... The realization that trouble was present, but so was God's mercy and grace provided me with the knowledge, that life is Good... It's about how I respond to the trouble that will determine if I am in trouble...

So I celebrate life while acknowledging it is not fair and I will have my fair share of trouble.

Prayer and poetry was my crutch...

Dedication

To my son, Tony (TJ) Jr. He is a gift from God, that helped me have the desire to transition in life.

To Jesus Christ who transformed my life.

To my mother who bared the burden of a troubled child.

To Leukemia for attacking my son and bringing my mind back into focus, about what really matters. Plus with evidence, my son can declare he's a warrior. My son through Jesus Christ won the battle...

Content

Makes life beautiful	7
The becoming of true self	9
No Mistaken Identity	10
The Process of living	11
Unified Soulfully	12
Draw From	13
Who Is	15
Moved by the Notable and Quotable	16
Life is Worth Living	17
Purposeful Tears	19
Mindset II	20
Available Everyday	21
Moments	22
Moments that Count	23
No Pity Party	25
Get Away	26
Dreams are Powerful	27
Like a River	28
? with a ?	29
Trusting the Beginning	31

Let There Be	33
Rescued...Now What?	35
Haunted by Shortcomings	36
Choose...Make the Choice	37
Sow in Love	38
Waiting is an Offensive Move	39
Watch Your Tongue	40
A Special Place	41
Affirmation	43
Disconnected	44
Identity	46
Out-takes	47
How We Finish	48
My Pledge	49
Reflecting	50
Did You Hear	52
Reason to Believe	53
All Across the Universe	54
Live Beyond the Past	56
Staying Humane	58

Makes Life Beautiful

The beautiful life
  that of striving
    that of struggling
      that of being counted out,
only to beat the odds
        Rising from the ashes
What a thrill
  what an adventure
    what an accomplishment.
No pity party
  No poor me
    No surrendering
to the frailties of fear

The beautiful life
  that of I shall be victorious
    that of I shall overcome
      that of I shall survive
Survive all misfortunes
  overcome all shortcomings
    triumph over all obstacles
What a mind-set
  What an outlook
    What an attitude

The beautiful life
   that of stepping outside the box
     that of following ones heart
        that of being true to self
With tears persevere
March with a warriors honor

Beautifully strive
Beautifully survive
Beautifully stay alive...

The Becoming of True Self

The features of my mind
is centered around betterment
The struggle of stepping beyond
 the limits of its' knowledge
Desiring to grasp the tools of understanding
so the wrench of wisdom will
    open other mental doors
  that lead to perfection
The man I visualize being
The greater man that speaks
   out   against my self-imposed
PAIN and AFFLICTION.
    YES! I want to be my conscience
the protector of my soul...
So when I say no one will harm me,
that includes my very own 'SELF'"

What courage it takes
to look in the mirror
see a stranger and vow
I SHALL GET TO KNOW YOU
nothing and no one shall stop me...
No more hiding I shall face me
with shame
admitting my denial
becoming un-pre-occupied with blaming others
for my shortcomings.

No Mistaken Identity

Simply me
wanting to be
simply me
a man of poetry
simply me
wanting to be
simply me
a spirited soul free
simply me
wanting to be
simply me
writing in harmony
simply me
wanting to be
simply me
a form of tranquility
simply me
wanting to be
simply me
no mistaken identity
just simply me...

Process of Living

There are many stages I travel
    witnessing the lightening strike
        hearing the thunder speak
            feeling the wind stampede
Going from pleasure to pain
    from happy to sad
        from relief to grief
Carrying my burden backpack
Looking for a sign of simplicity
Searching for a demonstration of love
Scouting for a path of peace
Questioning my very motives and reasons
    tired of being tired
        tired of falling short
           tired of chasing the wind
Constantly buying the grand illusion
Overlooking the signs of confusion
Creating a carnival of chaos
Kidnapping and holding love for an unknown ransom
NEVER SHALL I FORGET
where I was
where i was heading
where I've been
From grand illusion to nightmare to dream
    what an emotional ride
        what a mental expedition
           what a mindful adventure

Unified Soulfully

     Sing the song of life
the capturing of its beauty
based upon quality living
     Destiny with natural ingredients
a mind centered upon
  a peaceful journey
going beyond the passion of pleasure
  seeing the resting place
A place fit for angels
     transcending in tranquility
in between joy and excitement
  arriving from the past, the present
     the future
Generated
by the harmony
of existing with other forms of being
  founded by the necessities
of the heart in connection
to the standard of undeniable love

Drawn From

I've heard the ancient echoes
from moralist
      Philosophers
Everyday strugglers...
Each with their truths
   survival truths
      oppressive truths
         and sobriety truths
Where harmony was a stranger
      peace was an enemy
   and simplicity was leprosy
Yet there was moments
   moments of laughter
      moments of happiness
     and moments of rejoicing...

Those moments transpired
   only when the truth
  had its' moment in glory
Therefore, somewhere in time
   everybody can or have
      drawn strength
  from ancient echoes
Rather hypothetical
     rhetorical
    truth or myth
but we have nothing
   nothing to lose
if we find common ground
   become dream weavers
   and confusion wranglers

So in trying times
    we can keep on striving and smiling
Hearing those ancient echoes...

Who Is

Beyond a face
Lays feelings, emotions and thoughts
    All the above is true
Which reflect the life
The experience
    the known and unknown
that somehow is displayed
    without an identity or name
Then   BAM!
    Categorized
put in a cage
    A shell------a padded-room
Who is it?
    Not an open mind
Not an understanding heart
    and not a soul poor in spirit
Yes! beyond these actions
    the face remained
but the feelings, emotions and thoughts
Which reflect one's life
    The traditionalist

    The limitator The warden
    The solitude founder
Who Is It?
    Me, You or Them....

.

Move by the Quotable and Notable

The quotable: it goes without saying
The notable: the total eclipse of passion
    Activated from a yearning

The quotable: Larger than life
The notable: The existence of a soul-mate
    Motivated by the spiritual

The quotable: Highly recommended
The notable: A smiling face
    Inspired by kindness

The quotable: Count on me
The notable: the well never runs dry
    Influenced by experience

The quotable: It's loud and clear
The notable: Silent actions that speak in volume
Animated by one's purpose

The quotable and the notable
are creations of an outcome
that is rebirth..

Call it life
Give it any name you want
Living is a quotable
that leads to a notable
which gives an outcome...

Life is Worth Living

Here's to life and living
The road traveled
   and the road not taken
Here's to life and living
The story told
   and the story unspoken
Here's to life and living
The ups that's mourned
   and the downs that's celebrated
Here's to life and living
The until further notice love
   and the standing by for pain
Here's to life
A war
  a movement
    a frame of mind.

Here's to life and living
The thunder that stunned
   the lightening that marveled
The rained on parade
  the stormed on dream.
Here's to life and living
The ugly truth
   and the beautiful lie
Here's to life and living
The birth of
     the death of
the evolution of
   the crippling of

Here's to life and living
The slow and easy
    the fast and furious
Here's to life
A seed
  a season
    a frame of time...

The after hours of life
The after-taste of living

Here's to what life is/was given/giving
Here's to a life still worth living

Purposeful Tears

The truth of life
the seeds each and
everyone of us water
with tears of struggle
tears of inspiration
  tears of pain
    tears of joy
Each silent tear drop
holds a meaning
serves a purpose
has a destiny,
Which allows the spirit to soar
To soar through a dream
To ride upon a dream
A dream of tomorrow
that starts with today
that started with yesterday,
when silent tears   fell
fell casually down our face
reaching its' destination
watering the seeds of life
giving breath to a struggle
that evolved out of pain
making way to a testimony of inspiration
that built a heart of joy.
Never forget those tears
They are reminders
to remember the essence of ourselves
silently holding meaning
Let the tears flow....it's DESTINY

Mind-set II

I don't prescribe to happiness
My preference is Joy...

Happiness depends on what is happening
Happiness is a choice...

Joy is a state of being
A place in-spite of circumstances...

Life isn't Fair
we are born with a death certificate
So find one thing to rejoice about
each and everyday
which could be your last...

Available Every Day

Everyday is a good day
Another day to love
Another day to dream
Another day to be grateful
Everyday is a good day
A day to count your blessings
A day to dream of tomorrow
A day to see brighter skies
Everyday is a good day
For a smile is possible
For a dream is in reach
For a memory is created

Everyday is a good day
In the heart of harmony
In the mind of peace
In the eyes of enlightenment
Everyday is a good day
To be happy
To be hopeful
To be helpful...
So day after day
repeat tomorrow will be a brighter day
and say, nothing and no one
will stop it from being a GOOD DAY
See everyday is a good day!!!

Moments

Moments in time
I reflect upon memories
memories of joy
  memories of hope
So, in a moment of darkness
I have the courage and strength
to stand up under pressure,
continuing to walk by faith
Walking into the light
  the light of wisdom
    the light of knowledge
      the light of understanding
So, in a moment of chaos
I have inner-peace
Fearing not the man in the mirror
not letting circumstances
      dictate how i feel...
So, in a moment of time
I ask,
What has substance
  what holds meaning
    what if unaware of time
there's not a clock
there's not a calendar
It's the look of eternity
Moments collectively captured.!?

Moments That Count

A special moment
a time to remember
 a cherishable event or occurrence
like a day of holding hands
 a long good night kiss
maybe even the first kiss
 These are hallmark memories...

A special moment
 a moment that reflects love
life and quality living
 a time when peace was
nurtured in.
   A time when war was forgotten
race, creed nor religion
 had an effect...

A special moment
 a reflection of the
good-will, hopefulness and faith.
 Indeed a special moment
Visualize a peaceful journey
 the essence of a paradise
where knives are not needed
 guns never created
and poverty isn't known!

A special moment
A thought away
An act over the hill
A pleasant smile around the corner...

A special moment has happened
A special moment is going to happen!!!

No Pity Party

Feel sorry for me...I can not
Have self-pity...I will not
Fortunate I am...blessed I am
I could be in a worse situation
  I'm really not bad at all
Matter fact   my little is a lot
Though you look & say how bad
I'm living it, I'm glad...
Don't feel sorry for me
  I'm not feeling sorry for myself
How can I have self-pity
  when life is in me
    tragedy I think not
In the pit of despair
 I'm growing
    I'm living
Spiritually soaring
  Spiritually flourishing
God has granted me
  courage & inner-peace
I've found a sense of direction
 in a place where hopes and dreams
get smothered and drowned by the seconds.
complaint I can not
complaint I will not
Fortunate & Blessed I Am
Not because I Am, but because God is
The Great I AM
Do Not feel sorry for me...

Get Away

Let me get away from stress
Let me get away from everyday regrets
Let me get away
Let me have a brighter day
A day to read some poetry
as nature provides background harmonies
With my eyes seemingly closed
with the river tickling my toes...

Let me get away from conquer and destroy
Let me get away from guns being used like a toy
Let me get away
Let me have a brighter day
A day to lay naked with no insecurities
as the rainbow becomes my reality
Each color representing simplicity
A place I long to be...
Let me get away
Let me get away
Have a simple day away from doomsday
Let me get away and escape to explore
Let me get away and on this world close the door
Let me get away
Let me have a brighter day

Dreams are Powerful

Soaring through a dream
trying to find completeness
in and under a soulful pretense.
To let my spirit reflect
on subjects that others neglect.
Like the reality of a love that's real
knowing it goes beyond how one feels…

Soaring through a dream
to be at peace
erasing all my grief
so my mind can float on
with a delightful exploring song
getting deeply in-tune
sweeping turmoil away with a spiritual broom

Soaring through a dream
figuring out my vision
to live by a personal intuition
that will give me positive insight
while reaching greater heights

Some things can be accomplished
in our dream
let your dream capture you…

Like a River

Like a river
I flow sensing and feeling out
every object or living presence that I encounter

Like a river
I can cause panic and fear
when tested
and my course of direction is altered

Like a river
I can carry you on a peaceful journey
that is pleasant to the eyes
and comforting to the mind

Like a river
I have waves of reality
that must be took seriously and checked
before venturing into

Like a river I will not be stopped
through life obstacles
I continue
I continue to be like a river
flowing over or under
I am like a River..

? with a ?

They asked me questions
  How do you manage?
    How did you maintain?
As if i am working a miracle...
So their questions get questioned
  How could I not manage?
    How could I not maintain?
Both their questions and my questions
seemed to go un-answered...
But there is no mystery
  it is called inner-peace
the divine producer is the Creator
Yes Indeed
I know I make it sound simple
Yes...it is difficult
For those who seek instant peace
that is created by man
  concocted by hand
    relies on time and circumstance
      plus chance.
See everything within
  evolves to the outside
Therefore their search of simplicity
  should not be sought from the outer
The outer world...The outer world
  that uses weapon
  uses brutality, drugs
    and death threats to have peace.
These forms are destruction
Inner-peace draws from grace and mercy...

My answer come from within
So answer your own questions
why can't you maintain and manage.!?

Today my personal identity
questions their questions with a question
I refuse to let them cause me
to doubt my truth....

Trusting the Beginning

In the beginning.....I have no memory of
No memory of my own beginning
How I acted in my mother's womb
   there are no writings
     there are no recordings
If I was told how I behaved
I could not argue....it was not so
I could only say....I DON'T REMEMBER!

In the beginning....I have no memory of
No memory of coming out of my mother's womb
How I responded I don't have a clue
They said I cried...I DON'T REMEMBER THAT.!?
Did my mother scream...I ask cause I don't have no memory of that
So I can not say....it was not so.

In the beginning...I have no memory of
but I was and so it was
I am here now with no memory of my own beginning
There was a beginning
This is a truth I can argue

In the beginning with no memory
I believe or do not believe

Yet there was a beginning
There is a beginning I won't argue against
In the beginning God created

God created everything
The heavens, the earth
and all that dwell there within.
I don't have a memory of this
Yet, I cannot say it was not so
in the beginning...

The end is like the beginning.
In the beginning God knelt down
breathe the breath into man
and he became a living soul.

In the end the breathe of man is vacant.
that which he was given in the beginning.
the body is there and remains...
This is a truth I will accept

Let There Be

Let there be
    a place of grace
  And not one sad face
    where happiness rein supreme
  And not one unanswered dream....

Let there be
    a castle of celebration
  And not one false accusation
    with cheerfulness in every room
  And not on thought of doom....

Let there be
    a day of devotion
  And not one hour of commotion
    with brighter skies
  And not one action to criticize...

Let there be
    a year of loving cheer
  And not one month of fear
    when the mind can be at ease
  And not one deadly disease...

LET THERE BE
IS IN ACCORDS OF BEING
TOTALLY FREE!!!

SO LET THERE BE AND LET ALL SEE
WHAT COULD BE
A WORLD OF SUCH BEAUTY

IF WE
ONLY LET THERE BE

.

Rescued, Now What?

Who will rescue me
when my soul feels so empty
who will deliver me
when my spirit feel so lonely
who will unchain me
when bound by anxiety...

Isn't there this Jesus
who came to set the captives free
and yeah give sight to the blind
so their mind could see
give sound to the deaf
so they could hear clearly
Came down from heaven
to give life and life abundantly..
He died and rose all accordingly
Now the question is
how do I accept being free
how do I walk accordingly
to what has been purchased for me...

Haunted by Shortcomings

What am I not facing
Why run when no ones chasing
My thoughts need erasing
Cause Mercy and Grace
I seem not to be embracing
My addictions keep replacing
Temptation with sensation
My talents and treasures are wasting
Procrastination
it's holding hostage my elation
No jubilation
through this trumpeting tribulation
Yet
My soul urges me to face the nation
But
I'm not my own creation
Plus
My prayer life lacks communication
I do all the talking
That's a one way conversation
My mouth should suffer deflation
Cause my ego suffers inflation
and asking for help is like damnation

Choose....Make the Choice

Love like hate
is a dominating force,
Fear like faith
is a visible course...

The shocking
  the surprising
Can steal your voice,
The loving
  the faithful
is a cause to rejoice...

Faith expressing
itself through love
is a great choice...

Choose ye this day
to walk in Love...

Sow in Love

Moving in faith
operating in love
Speaking with a tongue
moist in proverbs
Touching with a hand
sweating in kindness
Seeing with eyes
wailing up in compassion
As I am mindful
of my own shortcomings
As I am conscious
of the favor I found
  the unmerited favor
    the unwarranted favor
Now my soul says yes
to being a blessing
  who shall I injure
    who shall I payback
There is nothing to gain
I sow in Love
and Reap joy and peace...

Waiting is an Offensive Move

What is this lapse of time
A twilight of some kind
participation....I wish to decline
but my mind is inclined
with no guideline nor promised sunshine
to journey on...in hope to find a sign
decode the orbiting suspense into divine...

so onward I march in a haze
fighting to still give the Almighty praise
though my heart is confused in this phase
The language of love has become a maze

I am amazed
cause I'm traditionally free
while philosophically...I'm under lock and key...
so I wait...this battle doesn't belong to me...

Watch Your Tongue

Be angry but sin not
Be humble not a hot shot...

Please don't give no one
a piece of your mind
You only use a small percent
and that's hard to find

so speak with the tongue of hope
hand out words that help others cope
truth without compassion is an overdose
It's like handing the hopeless person a rope...

so when angered try silence
and have no regrets
a kind word turns back wrath
and provides a safety net...

catch your self
or get caught...
bite your tongue
or pay the cost...

A Special Place

I look out upon the world
seeing much confusion and conflict
I don't want to share this
So I begin to write a script

Painting my world with emotions
Center my heart around love and compassion
knowing inner-peace sets the notion
that my mind can have satisfaction

I don't have to have fame
nor do I have to share the worlds shame
I won't play them black Friday games
Having salvation is my ultimate aim

Money, cars, jewelry, house
It can't help save my soul
Character, morals and love for God
is my one perfect goal

I care not what the world thinks of me
I'm a slave to the peace Jesus bought me
locked and brainwashed internally
Songfully full of praise I shall be

This is something the world
can't steal, murder nor abolish from me
My mind and heart is free
of the fantasy....getting stuff will make me...

Guess what....

surprise! I am somebody
where I need to be
where I want to be
he prepares a table for me
in the presence of my enemies
Now that is heavenly

Affirmation

A faith that won't falter
  A belief that won't shatter
    A hope that won't surrender

I'm still confident, I shall see the
goodness of the Lord in the land of the living...

My attitude is i shall not be defeated
  My weapons is prayer and praise
    My behavior is reflective

Victory comes not by my power and might
but by the spirit of the Lord...

Disconnected

There is something profound
about the lost and found
they've been unchained and unbound
Delivered from that propaganda
their smashing the prop
and scattering the ganda

Why?

Cause when there was no
sense of direction
no preferred affection
regulated rhetorical rejection.
out of Eternity
came heavenly perfection
radically rescuing
with love and correction.

Now on the rock the found stand
with a peculiar protection
No weapon formed
will conquer this connection

Death you say?

That's a false conclusion from a false illusion
there is a resurrection

Jesus rose and folded his clothes
taught and touched those chose
that's just a reflection.

He is the king of king and
Lord of lords...That's no suggestion
Therefor no voting both needed
God already held the election
So past, present and future presidents
can keep their hypothetic perspective
You can say that's hectic
but I'm in this world not of this world
This brother has been disconnected

Identity

I'm glad the world rejects me
It's Jehovah that I want to accept me
The Blood of Christ refresh me
His unfailing love protects me

Thank you God
you see the best me
Even when lust arrest me
Unworthy
yet you still bless me
How could I not profess thee

In Jesus I can be
that which God purposed me to be...
Child of the Most High God
is my identity...

Opportunity

In the shadow of all events
there's the light of opportunity
standing like a soldier
waiting for a die-hard command...

Lucky

Losers rely on luck
lucky people---where are they
You can't find them...
Fortunate is my brand of usage
Luck requires nothing of a person
Luck demands nothing of a person
Fortunate people work hard
and put themselves in position
to look like what some deem as luck....

Wish

A wish is a fish on dry land
No legs to walk to any
body of water.
Wishing is not for the able minded.
Please stop wishing and make it happen
Dream into ACTION

how we finish

The freedom song…I shall sing
I shall fly upon mercy's wings
Declare O'Death has no sting
On my knees I received grace from the king

Vow to living life my loyalty
No face no disgrace royalty
Even if they don't know of me
By the perplexing they'll let go of me

Announcing this one is different
Pronouncing this one is sent
He's a marathon not a sprint
To him the word of God is relevant

Now

Fighting the good fight of faith
I shall go the distant
It's not about the beginning
how we finish is most relevant

My Pledge

I Am a Citizen...I Have Rights!!!

I have a right to be delivered
    I have a right to be healed
        I have a right to cry tears of joy
    I have a right to shout victory
I have a right to profess things that are not as though they are
    I have a right to testify about my lord and savior Jesus Christ
        I have a right to speak words of encouragement
    I have a right to make a joyful noise unto the lord

I am a Citizen I have rights
I pledge allegiance to the blood of Christ

The Journey   The Life   This Adventure
On dry land there's a drought
On water there's a rising sea
In the air there's turbulence

The once gangster, the once hustler
The once thug, the want to be anything but me
The once down for whatever
I was creating storms I could not bare
On a canoe without a life jacket
On a plane without a parachute
In the desert without water

Young foolish, hopeless, helpless
No concept, No order
Headstrong without reason
Cocky without confidence
Arrogant without steam
Eager to be angry, quick to be frustrated
Swift to be bored, fast to be reckless
On the fast track to jail, grave and hell...

WOW! WOW! WOW!
Addicted, conflicted and afflicted
A dressed-up mess...jewelry-up jerk
Fashionably frustrated...

I suffered caught in a web of identity crisis
I suffered caught in a trap of worldliness
I suffered caught in a net of pleasure

    I suffered! I suffered!
I suffered out loud, I suffered inwardly
    I suffered self-affliction
I suffered misguided love
    I suffered! I suffered!
Looking and judging others for what they did
and didn't do
Blaming and expecting others to do that which I
couldn't do
    I suffered! I suffered!

The Path   The course   The race
Life more abundantly...

In the pit of despair...I cried out
In the sea of emotions... I screamed for peace
In the palace of pleasure...I desired tranquility
In the abyss of addiction...I sought God

Now! Now! Now!
This is only a moment
Half-way somewhere
The end of something that has begun
with
Reflections: A Mindful Journey!!!

Did You Hear

Prevalent and relevant is the word
It matters what you believe is not absurd
So I hope you heard...The WORD

What word?

The one that your not an accident
No bang! No Experiment!
No monkeying around
no such event...

Cause in the beginning
Everything was created...

Created on purpose with a purpose
for a purpose...
That includes You!!!

Reason to Believe

In a moment of reflection
My mind moves like a melody
with a thought of harmony
based on the verification of love
certified by how I treat me
which equates to my sound reason
to believe my tomorrows will be brighter...

Therefore

No purpose in remembering pain
unless it teaches the way of comfort
but to soak in it--that's non-sense
because there's love for every season
Desire it and devote yourself to peace
Making it the promise of your heart

All Across the Universe

Across the universe
Love is a demonstration
A form of behavior
The substance behind kindness
An act with actions of compassion
With many languages
With many good feelings
That inspire
That motivate
That stimulate...

See love is not blinding
Love is healing
Love is medication
No side-effect syndrome
Happy meal smiles
Happy memories beyond the clouds
Blue skies and
Star-lit nights...

This is universal
This is the beginning
And all that is in-between...

The gift of life
Was paid for by love
It's not racial
Not religious
Not territorial...

Such is love
Such is found everywhere
Such is our very own hearts

Slow down and listen
Then look.

It's everywhere
All across the Universe...

Live Beyond the Past

The journey of recovering is one thing
learning to live in recovery is everything
The royal understanding that I am great
A spotted past with a present clean slate

Different choices to make
Healthy decisions to celebrate
The serenity of sunshine I create
No room for doom to meditate
Living heavenly needs no rebate
Forgiveness is my resting place

Now

Someone else may whisper about the past
Then comes MY laugh,
hoping they catch whiplash

As they turn to see
what use to be
what use to abuse me
See the bruise me
Can't accept the new me
With this brand of Serenity
As peaceful is my New Identity

Still laughing cause
they thought so little of me
Because they thought
their own frailty
was hidden from me...

Anybody that is recovering from anything...Celebrate You...Don't let others just bring up the past of shame/addiction... Move to the overcoming, the bright future... Let them stay stuck... Keep it Moving... Move your mind and Conversation... Declare your new found lease on life along with your new identity...please

Staying Humane

Life is grand,
even when i don't understand
I am a mere man
with a worthy demand...

that

I learn to dance in the rain
Ride the storm of pain
Wrestle irrational thoughts to regain,
a mind that's prone for the insane...

So I make a conscious effort to
accept that which I can not change
It is I...The harmony hurricane
that looks to change
trusting the thunder of others
sounds strange

but

This conflict leads to gain
Peaceful is my new name
Perfection is not my claim
Being human is the aim
doing that which equates to liberty
plus the principle of that which is HUMANE...

There are more books to come:

A book of love letters called "***From the Heart Emotions Flow***"

A Devotional called: ***"Be Ye Separate"***

About Author

I have a bachelors degree in Human Services... I specialize in cognitive behavior therapy.

I am available to assist in journaling for healing. I can be reached at poeticallyyours360@yahoo.com or through my website that I blog on a weekly basis: thepoetic1.com/wordpress.

CPSIA information can be obtained
at www.ICGtesting.com
Printed in the USA
FFHW010415241218
49976228-54660FF